THE POWER OF A TESTIMONY

STORIES OF HOPE

LORI B. MOORE

TABLE OF CONTENTS

FOREWORD

"To everything there is a season; and a time to every purpose under heaven" Ecclesiastes 3:1

One thing is certain; Life is a journey, full of spiritual seasons.

As a case in point, several years ago I was asked by a person that is very dear to my heart, Linda Gilmore, to share my testimony at a seminar. I had never before shared my story in detail, but had given a short, three-minute version.

Since I knew that there are no coincidences with God, it suddenly dawned on me that He was answering a prayer I had recently been praying. I had been praying and asking Him to use me. I had told Him that I would be obedient to His call no matter what He asked. Little did I know at the time how much my life would be affected spiritually by my friend's request.

Linda is my spiritual mentor. I've learned many life lessons by watching her choose, time after time, to respond as Christ would when dealing with difficult situations. I am amazed at the strength of the godly character she possesses, as she has remained faithful and true to Him through all circumstances.

After Linda asked me to share, God began doing a work in my life. Year after year I had run from my past experiences instead of giving God the glory He deserved by sharing how He saved me.

By requesting my story, Linda unknowingly brought me to a place where I was faced with the decision to move forward and trust God, or once again retreat to my secret place – the place where no one knew my past.

I cannot express how thankful I am to you, Linda, as you have encouraged me and loved me unconditionally. It is because of you that I began to spend precious time with the Father as He guided me in writing my testimony.

It is the Lord who has led me to comprise this book, because He wants people to come to know Him intimately and to hear stories of His grace and mercy.

So Miss Linda, full of beauty and grace, and my sweet friend: I dedicate this collection of women's testimonies, The Power of a Testimony, to you, and pray that these life stories will touch many hearts. May each person who reads these personal recollections realize the rich abundant life God desires for each and every one of His children.

PREFACE

Having been a teen mom my goal in sharing my testimony is to reach teens before they make the same poor choices I did, and to show them insight into how God has a plan and a purpose for their lives.

Teens of today are our leaders for tomorrow. They need encouragement, especially from those of us that are older. We've lived out our teenage years, and they look to us to be authentic and real with our life stories so hopefully they can learn from our mistakes.

Another equally important goal in sharing is to alert parents to several key factors that have an influence in their child's life choices. Parents play a huge roll in supporting their children to make the godly choice not to allow an unplanned pregnancy in their life.

Parents have been given children as a gift from God and it is our responsibility to live mature and godly lives as examples for our youth. We must realize how our actions mold our kids to make healthy godly decisions when they're older.

The Power of a Testimony includes real authentic stories of the lives of several women of different ages that have come together to comprise this book. Most of us are members of the same church, Long Hollow Baptist Church in Hendersonville, TN., with the exception of Stephanie W. who attends a different church.

Our goal is to step forward and share our life situations in order to bring the shameful darkness of abuse and sin into the glory and forgiveness of the light of God.

I believe that truth needs to be revealed, and that the shame and pain of sin will never be vanquished if left in the dark.

This book includes my testimony and reveals the hard facts of teen pregnancy and the life-changing consequences of it.

Stephanie W.'s story reveals the fear and self-loathing caused by sexual abuse early in her life and how food, alcohol, and sex played a role in her desperate search for healing.

There are more short testimonies such as Gaby Overall's story of the death of her father at age twelve, and how this caused her to spiral downward until God worked in her life to help her deal with her pain and loss.

Andrea Huddleston's story reveals the hardship of growing up in a home filled with insecurity, turmoil, arguing, and constant change.

Kaden's Story by Terri Hagood gives a glimpse of God at work in the life of a Christian family as they sought God's will for a precious little boy who was the baby son of a prison mom.

In So Proud Terri Hagood gives a short testimony of her love and admiration for her daughter as she witnessed her daughter's strength in helping her friend choose life, not abortion for her unplanned pregnancy.

In Allyson Hagood's testimony, Stephanie's Story, she shares how her faith in God gave her the strength to confront a friend who was considering aborting her unplanned pregnancy – and the amazing outcome of her friend's choice.

Rhonda Ponessa's testimony is an inspiring one, filled with people and events that shaped her faith as she grew up the niece of a country music legend.

I've also included a poem and narrative I wrote that shares how the Holy Spirit stays close by our side to reveal to us hope, humility, and self-acceptance.

In the poem "The Master's Plan", it deals with the life-long pain and regret of abortion and how God heals those that turn to Him for forgiveness.

Lastly, the most important goal we have in sharing our stories is to acknowledge God, for His love is real! He teaches, encourages, and guides us as we grow in His love and find purpose, peace, and meaning in the glorious plan He has for our lives!

THE POWER
OF A TESTIMONY

LORI B. MOORE

THE POWER OF A TESTIMONY
BY LORI MOORE

Chapter One: I remember that day .....

It was late on a Thursday afternoon when I begrudgingly entered the mall. One week before Christmas, I must have been crazy to wait so late to finish my shopping.

As I hurried from store to store, I couldn't help but notice the young girl walking in front of me. She was dressed in jeans and wore a beautiful red Christmas sweater with black boots.

Something about her was different. I didn't know why I was drawn to her and kept staring at her. She seemed so young, yet she seemed to have an older more serious nature about her than most teens, at least she didn't seem to have the same quick happy-go-lucky skip in her step.

She had long blonde hair pulled back in a ponytail that bounced back and forth as she walked.

An item I had been searching for caught my eye, and as I turned to go into the store I couldn't help but be distracted when two young teens walking on the other side of the mall suddenly ran through the shopping crowd to the girl in front of me and hugged her.

"Hi! We haven't seen you in so long. How are you and how are you feeling?" they asked.

"Oh, I've been doing well. So far, so good. Hey, when is Christmas break? I really miss you, you know," said the girl.

"We miss you too. You wouldn't believe how busy we are and how crazy it is now. All in all, though, high school senior year is fun! Well, we have to run, so much to do. It was so good to see you," they said as they disappeared into the crowd.

"Same here!" she answered back. Then it happened. She turned to enter the store and I saw that she was heavily pregnant. Time seemed to stand still, and my thoughts immediately took me back to a time long ago.

She must have looked the same as another girl I had once known. The girl I remembered was also young and pregnant. The girl I remember was me!

She watched her friends disappear as they continued on with their lives in high school without her there to join them.

"Oh no," I thought. I felt an overwhelming sadness for her as she watched them hurry on with their shopping, laughing and carefree.

She turned and saw me looking at her, and for a moment I wanted to go to her and put my arms around her.

I knew her pain and sadness and I watched as she put down her head. It seemed to me that she was crying, but she gathered herself and moved on.

That day in the mall was a day of significance for me, and I realized that God had placed the girl in my path for a purpose. The sight of her brought me back to the memory of my teen pregnancy, and I could hardly bear the pain. Seeing the girl brought back all the emotions I had felt during that time long ago. Still, I wasn't exactly sure why God was doing this to me.

"Okay Lord, you have my complete attention! But, when will I be able to get past the pain I feel every time I see a young pregnant girl? I asked.

It was then that I realized for the first time in my life I felt a calling. The thought entered my mind, maybe if I share my painful experience with other youth they would think twice before it was too late.

"Okay, Lord, I'm beginning to understand. Could it be that my story could help others? Could it really make a difference? I've only told a handful of my friends. What will they think of me?" I thought.

"Alright Lord, now I'm scared to death and don't really understand what's happening , but I will do whatever You want me to do. I can't do this alone. You have to do it!

"This is what it must mean to give a personal testimony and I think I'm finally ready to share mine, so show me what You want from me and how to do it," I said to Him in a breath prayer.

Chapter Two: Before I begin, let me tell you what I believe

So much of our life is spent trying to accomplish something worthwhile, only to find that we end our endeavor empty handed, finished before we've even begun, and have just wasted time.

We have many wonderful dreams when we're young, but as we get older, we get caught up in mundane activities that leave us tired. We realize we can't do much more than just get by, let alone believe in ourselves, step out, and orchestrate a meaningful and wonderful event.

Satan, the enemy, has us exactly where he wants us when this happens. He wants us to feel defeated whenever we step out of our comfort zone and step up to the plate for God. He reminds us of our failures, and we begin to think we have nothing worthwhile to offer.

But, when we choose God as our heavenly Father, He knows a much different ending to our life story. He plans for us, in our insignificance, to have the ability through Him to accomplish more than we could ever dream possible.

When I was a young child, I remember watching the movie The Ten Commandments. It was based on the story of Moses. God had chosen him to lead His people out of slavery in Egypt, and it showed what it must have been like to experience the ten plagues God sent to persuade the Pharoah Ramses to free His people. The plagues were shown in frightening detail. I'll never forget how terribly real the depiction of the angel of death was as it came in the night to take the first born of those who had not placed lamb's blood on the door post.

I thought Moses seemed larger than life, and was amazed at how it must have taken incredible faith and courage for him to obey God's call and complete such an unimaginable assignment. I'm still awe struck at how much was accomplished through him for God's Kingdom.

Moses was given a command by Almighty God, he chose to obey and trust God, and God worked through him to accomplish His divine plan.

When I was young I didn't fully understand that it was God who worked through Moses to accomplish His purposes. The kind of Biblical faith and courage he had were spiritual mysteries to me. I thought that the people of the Bible were different, not "normal". I imagined they were superhuman heroes.

What would you say if I told you that you, too, have a great story to tell? Your story is as real as the story of Moses, and it takes place during your lifetime. It is just as dynamic, and it tells of the love of God and what happened when you chose faith in Him and were redeemed. The title of your story is called "Your Testimony", and God desires for it to be shared with others.

Try to imagine that when you gave your life to Christ and asked Him to be Lord of your life, you had a one-on-one, intimate moment with the creator of the universe. He became your daily guide, living within you as only the Holy Spirit can, and anything and everything about you was transformed at that moment in time. You became a new creature-, a creature that could do all things through Christ.

Moses was an ordinary, sinful man whose life was made extraordinary by the power of God living within him. His story is one of many in the Bible that give us a glimpse of the love of Almighty God, the kind of love that is like none we could ever imagine. His love is undeniable, unconditional, and complete.

When we let our salvation experience sink in, come to know Him, and begin our new life in Him, often we ask, "What could I possibly do for You, Lord, to ever repay you for saving my life? What could I do in my lifetime to make a difference?"

The thought of my life making a difference for God empowers me and at the same time frightens me. I begin to think that I will fail because nothing in me or about me could ever hold the power to impact others or to have eternal significance.

But, the answer to those questions is simple; yes, there is something we all can do. Through the gift of our personal testimony, God can work in us and through us to help others.

There is power in our testimony. When we share it with others, we access the supernatural power God provides whenever we give Him glory. We help others make choices, and God changes their circumstances to reveal His purpose and plan for their lives. He takes away the guilt that overshadows lives and gives the freedom experienced when He is given full authority over our lives and is acknowledged as our Lord.

We have a chance to make a difference in the world for Christ by acknowledging how He's changed us. All this can be accomplished by sharing it with someone who needs to hear it.

Yes, it's true that it is not necessary for us to tell our story to others in order to be given the gift of salvation. But by doing so we show the depth of God's love and connect with another human being that has had the weight and worries of sin in their lives, just like us.

I ask you, "If you had the opportunity to share how God gave you the freedom from sin by sharing how He has forgiven you and given you peace and love, why wouldn't you use this incredible God-given tool to do so? What action on your part could be more important?"

The truth is, we forget we are unable to do any more than simply share our salvation story. We are to trust God with the rest, because only He can give the gift of salvation. We share what God has done in our lives and He works through us to connect to the hurting heart of another and hope that they choose His transforming love.

Chapter Three: The Testimony

Our personal testimony is a true gift, and it is meant to be shared. It is a sincere way to show others how God stepped into our lives and changed us, and a great way to share Christ with others. When thought of in this way, we begin to see that the example of our lives, and who we have become through Him, can make a difference for His glory.

It's hard to open up and witness to others; it shouldn't be, but it is. We must remember that if we feel a deep connection to someone who may be going through the same trial we went through, this is not a coincidence. God, in His perfect timing, has placed that person in front of us so we might join Him in His work, step out of our comfort zone, and share with another who needs Him. They may desperately need us to care! We must never underestimate the importance of this.

Every testimony is different. For some, the circumstances of their story are beautiful. For others they are not. Remembering the mistakes I had made in my life always ushered in feelings of sadness and deep shame. I'd spent most of my life trying to hide from the "me" back then because I was afraid no one would accept me if they knew the real me.

Now I know this is how Satan tries to keep me "stuck" and ineffective for God. He's a lying, abusive creature that wants us never to think we're important to God- not us; God would and could never work in and through us.

But, God has reminded me that no matter how painful and shameful my story is, He has forgiven me- plain and simple. As far as the east is from the west, that's how far He has removed my sin.

The truth is, the gift God gave me, the gift of eternal life and forgiveness, was bought at a price, a price unimaginable- His death on a cross, for you, for me, for all if we believe in Him.

After many years of going back and forth wondering if I should share or not, I have made a decision for the Lord that I will stand strong in His promises and be willing to share my testimony. For so many years I knew I had to start somewhere, but didn't. I asked myself time and again, what on earth was I waiting for?

It's ironic how excited I was to share other aspects of my life, but to tell you the truth I put sharing my testimony off because I would tell myself that it wasn't necessary to open up the closet of my past. Now that it is behind me, why did I need to bring up old hurts?

The Lord knew I wanted to, but He also knew I hadn't fully forgiven myself. I held on to my past, and by doing so, I held onto my sin. My faith was not where it should have been. I didn't fully give up control and held God at arm's length.

Once again, Satan knew that as long as he tried to convince me to hold onto my shame, he would render me ineffective for God.

Now, I have given God the burden of my past, and know that I will not forget my sin, but it will no longer enslave me. His love delivers us from the shame of our past, but we must get to the point where we can say, "I'm ready to let go, Lord, of the chains. I'm ready to turn a new chapter, and I allow You to transform me. Now is the time I have finally chosen to live an authentic life for You!"

Chapter Four: Sin and Consequences

We all make mistakes; we are human and "in the world." We painfully watch our children learn the hard way how to make wiser choices. Often we realize that we, too, revert back to our old ways of learning the hard way, just like when we were children.

How many times do we find ourselves saying," Why did I do that? Why did I say that? Why did I think that?"

Let's face it, we are daily capable of choosing the wrong path and making devastatingly poor and sinful choices that can change the course of our lives forever. Think, for a moment, of the millions of people sitting in our prisons who because of one wrong choice, are spending the rest of their lives serving a sentence behind bars.

We have to die to ourselves daily and confess our sins; for as long as we are on this earth, there will be struggles over sin.

We make bad choices in our lives that change and alter our lives forever. Sin is a powerful thing, and Satan desires to grab hold of us, making us feel defeated with no way out.

But, I tell you this, "Our Heavenly Father is so much more powerful! He is the God of the universe!" Take a moment to let that fact sink in, and to remember, "All things are possible with Christ!"

If we have done the unthinkable, only God can take our poor choice, turn it around, and make it work to bring Him glory.

That's right, He can and will take our sins, and the terrible consequences it has had in our lives, turn our story around and make it a bestseller, a life "story" that when shared can and will make a difference. It will be a success story beyond any you could ever imagine.

He desires for us to give him our "mess-ups", and when we "own up" and come to Him in humbleness, He gives us His mercy, grace, and love. It truly is that easy.

Remember this: sometimes, the most painful moments of our lives teach us the most; only then do we "get it". We grow wiser from our mistakes. It's never, ever too late to take the right way- the way of Christ.

Oddly enough, looking back, I wouldn't change my story. It is because of it that I am who I am today. God, in His incredible timing, allowed me to fall. He watched as I fell deeper and deeper into sin, despair, and depression.

Remembering back on these times, I can only imagine how my Heavenly Father must have felt as He watched me from heaven. I imagine Him waiting for the moment when I surrendered and called out to Him.

My husband once shared a dream he had, and I was so moved by it that I will never forget it. In the dream, he was in water filled with high waves, and it became harder and harder to swim. He realized that he was losing strength, and he went under again and again. Soon he realized he was not going to make it.

Just when he could swim no more, he called out to God to save him. It was at this moment a strong arm appeared from above and grabbed hold of him. Looking up, he saw Christ on the cross, and Christ's right arm lifted off the cross and reached down to save him. He said the look on Christ's face was one of incredible love.

I get shivers every time I think of this, because my husband's dream had shown clearly what Christ does every time we cry out to Him. He rescues us no matter what circumstances existed in our lives at the moment we made the decision to make Him Lord of our lives. All salvation experiences are special and incredible moments in time. They are so special that the angels in heaven rejoice.

If we can put our trust in the one who gave His life for us so that we might be saved by calling on His powerful name, then we can never forget our testimony. We are called to share our love and experiences. When we accept Christ, He pours His love into us. We have only to reach inside and access His love, His power. It's then that He will give us strength and courage. Not our own strength, but strength that comes from Him- supernatural strength to make it through.

Chapter Five: My Story

If you see me now, you may think that I have it pretty much together. I attend church regularly, have a family that I love dearly, and have a wonderfully happy life.

You may not know that there was a time in my life long ago when it was a much different story.

At sixteen years of age I, by making a foolish choice, became pregnant. No girl thinks that something like that would ever happen to her, but that's exactly what happened to me the summer before my senior year in high school. Because we were irresponsible, my boyfriend and I were faced with the reality of an unplanned and unexpected teen pregnancy.

Chapter Six: Why does a girl allow herself to get pregnant? What factors are involved?

Even though teens are ultimately responsible for the choices they make, there are factors that can and do influence a son or daughter whether or not they make the godly choice not to allow an unplanned pregnancy in their lives.

Parents, this is where your extremely important role comes into play in your teen's life, especially when they become of the age to say yes or no to engaging in sex.

Let's face it, nothing can ever prepare you for hearing the word "pregnant" when it involves your child. "Devastating and life-changing" are two words I think best describe the experience.

I know that I am not an educator or a doctor. The factors I am listing are but a few from a list of so many, and many are my opinion. Let's get real and be honest now, because we as parents want to do anything and everything to prevent our children from becoming pregnant.

Why do teens allow a pregnancy to happen? We prepare them for the teen years and all that comes with it, but still some succumb to the pressure of sex, and ultimately someone we know becomes pregnant.

I've listed several possible factors parents may contribute negatively in the family setting which could lead to predisposing their teen to become pregnant:

- You knew you had to tell your son and daughter about sex, but because you were too uncomfortable to say the words, you didn't

- You sensed your son or daughter was becoming promiscuous, but again you buried your head in the sand and hoped the problem would simply go away

- Your teen watches the wrong types of movies that are too sexually explicit and they listen to songs that seem to encourage young love and sex, and you haven't questioned it

- You and your husband used to spend time with your teen, but lately you've quit spending time with them. Or Dad, you used to spend time with your little girl, but now that she's becoming more grown up and a women you're not as comfortable with her. That needs to change, because she needs you now more than ever! You are her role model and an example of what she should look for in a husband. It's time the two of you went on Daddy-Daughter dates, because she needs to know that she'll always be Daddy's little girl

- Perhaps you've become a mom and dad that constantly fight. Your daughter feels like she's caught in the middle, or the cause of your fights

One of you is having an affair, and there's so much tension at home that perhaps it's become so unbearable that your daughter subconsciously will do whatever it takes to get away, even allow herself to get pregnant!

You used to be a church-going family, but now you don't go. You stopped doing family things altogether, but you must take the time! Your family's the most valuable gift from God.

These are just some of the factors. According to a recent article from Pregnancy RX - Your Trusted Source, it states that " young people are experimenting with sex at an earlier age which seems to be a major factor leading to teen pregnancy. Teens that are sexually active have reported that they felt pressured by their friends or partners to have sex before they were ready. Drugs and alcohol use also lowers inhibitions in teens and may contribute to many cases of unplanned sexual activity. There is a strong link to teen pregnancy, sexual abuse, and rape. 60% of girls who had their first sexual experience before the age of 15 say that they were forced the first time. Girls who have a history of being molested and abused sexually have been shown to be more likely to be sexually promiscuous as teens.

Studies show that over half of all teen mothers who are or were in abusive relationships with the babies' fathers are beaten and the fathers try to control every aspect of their lives.

Teen boys and girls who witness or experience domestic violence in the home are more likely to become teen parents.

Girls whose fathers leave the home when they are very young start having sex at a younger age and have a greater chance of becoming teen moms.

There are many problems for teen moms. Most live in a state of poverty and are far less likely to pursue their education. This limits the number of careers open to these young mothers and reduces their chances of ever getting out of poverty.

Problems for the child have been found to have a higher rate of learning disabilities and behavior problems at school. The drop out rate of children of teen moms is much higher. One of the possible reasons for this poor academic performance is a lack of stimulation from the mother during the child's infancy. The moms often wish they could continue with their own lives and care for a baby later in life, but the facts are now they have a child who needs them.

There are many problems for the family of a teen mom. Children naturally look up to their mom, wanting to do what they did in life. Often sons of teen moms get a young girl pregnant. They place less importance on getting an education and finding a good job which would allow them the chance of a better life, and a cycle begins to be passed down through the years of more and more unplanned pregnancy.

The only program that really works is abstinence.

Chapter Seven: Shamed beyond belief!

Shamed beyond belief I buried my head in my hands and sobbed when I found out the news that I was pregnant.

Why did I do this?

Since I have listed some of the common factors in the previous chapter, let me say that there were some of these factors occurring in my life at the time I got pregnant. Concerning my pregnancy, this is all I will reveal because it is far too important to me that I not share my testimony at the risk of hurting others I love. For my experience, and after much prayer, I have chosen not to reveal all of the details and I hope the reader will understand. I do hope, however, that teens and parents will read the risk factors and know what to look for in their own lives so they may prevent a pregnancy from happening to someone they love.

Chapter Eight: My story

I was brought up in a Christian home. I had been baptized at age eleven, and loved to go to church and listen to the preacher and his message. By all accounts, I had always tried to do the right thing and was an honest, caring person.

Nothing can ever prepare you for the news that you are pregnant.

I will never forget the tears my mom and dad shed when I told them the news. Remembering back on those days, I see how my parents tried to make the best of a bad situation, and stood by me.

One hot summer afternoon, my dad was swinging on the porch with me, and he said, "Honey, you know you don't have to go through this. There is a way out." He was speaking of abortion, and I must admit that through my tears I was desperate to have a way out.

He had so many wonderful aspirations for his daughter, and loved me, as did my mother. I knew it was the only way he could think of at the time to help me, and somehow it eased my pain to know my dad would suggest something so incredibly unacceptable simply because he loved me so.

I mentioned this to my boyfriend, but he said that by no means would we ever do that. He said we would get married, and we did. I've since thanked him for standing strong and helping me keep my head on straight at a time when I was so in shock.

We were married for eleven years, and even though we've since divorced and remarried others, he is still a friend. So many teenage marriages, especially ones brought together by teen pregnancy, don't make it. It's unbelievably hard to be a child and have a child; that's the sad and tough reality of it. At a time in one's young life when you should be having fun, being responsible for another life can be overwhelming.

Children are a gift from God and deserve to have parents with the ability and maturity to handle the trials that come from being a parent. Children cannot choose who their parents are and shouldn't receive anyone other than loving devoted moms and dads.

Some amazing parents have had their children young, but all too often the dreams teen parents have of going to college and having a fairy-tale wedding are soon dropped by the wayside when they find that they are going to be parents. They hear the cries in the night by their helpless little one, and quickly their thoughts turn to wondering how on earth they are ever going to be able to care for a baby.

When we were married, it wasn't the kind of wedding a young girl dreamed of with bridesmaids, flowers, and her father giving her away in marriage. Instead, we stood in the county courthouse and said our vows with our parents standing behind us inwardly crying. We began our new life the best we knew how.

We tried to take it one day at a time. I didn't know then how much the shame of the sin and poor choices I had made would take such a terrible toll.

Chapter Nine: What the world wants us to believe

Today, television and movies portray young love, teen pregnancy, and having sex before marriage as somehow glorified or romanticized. They don't often tell the "real story"- that more often there are heartaches and hard times.

For this reason, I hope others will read my story and learn from it. In telling my story, I will not overly dramatize the facts or withhold emotions, because it is too important to tell the real events and show the real pain associated with it.

As God as my witness, I pray that He will give me the words to share so that those reading it will know how He saved my life. My wish is for no one to be harmed by reading these words, and instead I pray for compassion and understanding.

Most of all, when the time is right after a man and woman are married, if they find they are expecting a baby, it should be a time of rejoicing, not a time filled with sorrow and regret.

Chapter Ten: The Pregnancy

At sixteen years of age, my Dr. informed me that a teen-age pregnant girl is at a higher risk for a condition known as pre-eclampsia. This condition is characterized by dangerously high levels of blood pressure and can often be fatal to mother and child if not medically monitored and treated.

I, having been healthy most of my life, had never experienced an illness that required bed rest and medication, but I developed this condition early in my pregnancy. I didn't have symptoms when my blood pressure would rise to dangerous levels. Often for no apparent reason it would do so. My doctor kept a close watch on me, and quickly placed me on strong medication which made me sleepy.

I'm thankful that although my husband and I were young and poor (often another reality of teen pregnancy), and although we had to go to a special clinic for expectant parents who were unable to pay the high costs of a pregnancy, I had a wonderful doctor who was caring and non-judgmental. Most important, he was a Christian and he prayed for me.

As a sixteen year old pregnant girl, often I was shunned. This was especially the case with older strangers and some of my friend's moms. This "predicament" wasn't accepted then and is not today. You were labeled a bad girl if you became a pregnant teen. Prejudices have been somewhat softened, but not completely. Nothing, however, changes the fact that there are consequences to sin.

During my pregnancy my friends had a bridal and baby shower for me. This was such a kind thing for them to do and it really made everything easier for me at first. But as the months rolled on I only recollect a handful of friends calling or coming to see me. This was the time my husband and I needed our friends the most, but I understood that they were busy with their lives and in school.

It's an awkward time for a pregnant teen; she doesn't fit in with other moms who are usually much older, and she doesn't fit it with her friends.

As the time grew closer to my due date, my doctor became more and more worried about my condition and made the decision to induce labor early. My daughter was born two weeks early.

She entered the world; all 6.lbs. 9 oz. of her with a head full of beautiful white blond hair. She made her entrance in a sleepy, somewhat drugged state due to the medications I had taken throughout the pregnancy.

Three days after delivery, I went home to my parent's house. This was a chance I had to receive much needed help and have time to rest, but I was so ashamed of my predicament I hated to ask for help. This is not what a new mother should do. There are many sleepless nights dealing with the demands of a newborn, and one should accept as much help as possible until she is strong enough to take care of her baby.

Looking back, I realize that I had been given medication to sleep for five months, and I went from sleeping most of the time, to not getting much sleep after my baby arrived; just as all new moms and dads do. I also know now that I was punishing myself by not asking for help. I know that sounds crazy, but I hated to bother anyone anymore than I already had by asking for help.

It was at this time that I began fighting another terrible symptom of shame and fatigue; depression. Depression from the thoughts I had of the crushing disappointment and embarrassment I had caused my parents.

Remembering back, I see clearly that I was also vulnerable to extreme attacks from Satan.

I was worn out, exhausted, ashamed, and alone most of the time, I was also a recipe for disaster of epic proportions.

Soon I was in the fight of my life, and it was a fight that Satan was determined to win.

Chapter Eleven: Dangerous Depression

So many things were out of control in my life at this time. I tried as hard as I could to fight it, but a terrible depression came over me. Day after day I spent most of my time alone with my baby, and more often than not I would cry.

The depression was more than the baby blues; it had developed into a terrifying sense of foreboding and self-hatred. Satan began using the depression as a tool to destroy me. He knew how vulnerable I was, and he began to pierce me deeply with his destructive arrows.

I had not been to church since my pregnancy. I felt like I had become the "talk" of everyone. Gossiping mouths seemed to find pleasure in my situation. The subject of pregnancy wasn't talked about, and most tried to kept a secret.

I felt as if I couldn't talk to anyone about my feelings. Once school started back in September, I wasn't allowed to go my senior year. This rule was common place. I felt as if some now looked upon me as a bad influence and turned away.

It was very hard on my husband as well. He got the best job he could and tried to financially support his family. Teen pregnancy is a tough thing for a young teen father as well.

Often the father abandons the mother and child, and the mother is forced to raise the child by themselves. It's sad how an irresponsible father can simply go on with his life as if nothing happened. I was fortunate to have a husband who did the best he could and devoted himself to his wife and child.

There were so many changes in my life; one day practicing cheerleading in the summer to the next morning getting sick from morning sickness. One day living life happy-go-lucky, and the next my life as I knew it was changed forever.

I was isolated and alone most of the time, which isn't good in any situation. I cannot explain how I felt, other than to say that days and nights began to blend into one and I lost my appetite and needed help desperately.

Worst of all, I had learned to become an actress, smiling on the outside, but terrified on the inside.

I had strange thoughts that made me feel like a monster. I knew this wasn't normal, but didn't know what to do. I felt like I would never be right again. These are not the feelings a mother should feel. How could I ever be a good mother if I was such a worthless and terrible person?

Chapter Twelve: Saved by grace

Hopefully, by being completely transparent, I pray that what I am sharing will prevent another from going through the same. Although the horror and heartache of an attempted suicide is one of the most desperate measures one can ever resort to, it shows the extent of my deep depression. It is also what can happen to a person when they are out of the will of God and in the grip of sin.

All that I now share is the culmination of so many factors that were in my life at that time. I needed help and needed God most of all.

According to what my gynecologist later told me, I had been dealing with one of the most severe cases of depression that can come over a new mother, and I had needed immediate intervention and help. He said that it is only by the grace of God that I am alive today.

Day after day, I struggled. I was amazed that no one could see what was happening to me. I wanted to tell someone, but I never allowed anyone to see what was really going on behind closed doors.

I felt that I had made such a mess of everyone's life. I felt that my baby deserved to have a "normal" mom, not the strange, sick, shameful one I had turned out to be. I thought, If I could just disappear, then everyone would be so much better off than they were now...

I began to methodically plan my exit from the excruciating pain I felt. I thought if I were gone, it wouldn't be bad for my husband, my baby, and my family. I felt like this was the only way my family could get over the harm I had caused. After all, I was the reason for so much pain and hurt.

As I write these words, I feel such compassion for the girl I was then. I know that I wasn't thinking in a rational way, but instead I was focused on what the depression was making me think and feel. Oh, how I shudder at the emotions brought on by this disease. I know now I was desperately trying to fix the problem; to control the situation. I was depending on myself instead of trusting in God.

My focus was twisted. Instead of reaching out to my family, I was too messed up to do so and stayed focused on the wrong things. I couldn't understand my feelings and was terrified by them.

I know it was my responsibility to make the right choices in my life, but looking back, I also see that I was sixteen years old when I married, and my husband was eighteen; we were still kids ourselves. Though this is true, I still take full responsibility for having not chosen the right actions.

The truth is, at this sad moment in my life Satan wanted me to fail; he wanted nothing more than to destroy me, and he almost succeeded.

I believe with all my heart that he was working to bring me down, and because I had turned from God, Satan thought he could win.

Chapter Thirteen: Amazing grace, How sweet the sound, He saved a wretch like me

I knew I could not go on any longer. I was getting worse. Most of all, I knew my baby deserved so much more than what I could give. That was the day I decided there was no other way out than to leave. I had lost all strength and will to live.

I decided to borrow my mother's car, and I told her I needed a break and wanted to go shopping.

I called my mother-in-law and asked if she would keep my baby for the day.

I packed the diaper bag full of extra diapers, food, and baby clothes. I held my baby, told her I loved her and she didn't deserve anything but the best in a mom. I felt sick, and with a lump in my throat I told her that one day I hoped she would understand.

I drove to my mother-in-law's house and said good-bye, then drove back to our home and proceeded to take a bottle of pain pills I had been given when I had wisdom teeth removed a year earlier.

I laid down on the sofa, covered myself with a blanket, and simply went to sleep....

The next thing I remembered, I was in the emergency room throwing up. I could hear voices saying, "It's another suicide attempt."

Then, next I remember I was in the intensive care unit attached to many tubes, and then I blacked out again.

The next day, I was awakened by a kind, gentle nurse who held my hand and told me I had so much to live for; she knew I had a husband and a beautiful baby. She told me God loved me and would help me.

In an instant, I drew my hand back, and glared at her saying, "You don't know what I've done! You don't know who I am or know anything about my life!" I turned my head away from her feeling disgusted that I had somehow lived and my plan hadn't worked.

She wasn't at all deterred by my anger, but instead she told me she knew I needed rest and that I was going to get through this.

My internist made a visit, and all he said was, "I'm releasing you from the hospital in two days and you'll be just fine." Just fine? I thought how on earth am I going to be just fine? I have never been more frightened than I was at that moment. I had never felt so alone; so lost. I had no idea what to do next.

My parents came to visit and I lied, put on my best face, and told them I had had a drug reaction. They believed my story, and the next day they drove me to their house; the home where I had been raised.

Chapter Fourteen: The moment when He reached down from heaven and lifted me from my despair

As soon as I got home, I went into the bathroom and closed the door. I started to cry uncontrollably and fell to the cold, hard tile floor. I remember looking up, and for the first real time in my life, I spoke out to God and pleaded, "Lord, please help me. I cannot sink any lower. Please, please help me."

What I'm about to say, you may choose not to believe. The fact is, a miracle happened on that day. Maybe you don't believe in miracles from God, but I know that at the moment I spoke out to Him, He heard my cries and reached down to save me- to heal me.

I felt a warm sensation from the top of my head to my toes, and it was as if someone was lifting me up from the floor. I couldn't believe what was happening. I stood there that day looking at my reflection in the mirror, and I began to feel different. I looked out the window and saw the colors of the flowers and the trees, and I realized I had not seen color or tasted food in such a long time. I had been so depressed that it had been impossible to do so.

I began to dry my tears, and became overwhelmed with joy. I couldn't wait to pick up my baby. I hurried to her, picked her up, and held her close. I laid her on the bed and watched her sleeping. I slowly removed her blanket and went over every inch of her body. I counted her fingers and toes, picked her up again, and smelled her hair. I began to thank God for His love, over and over I said the words, "Thank you, Lord, for saving me. Thank you. Thank you for this beautiful baby! Please forgive me. I'm so sorry, Lord."

I was amazed that it was as if all that had happened had been a bad dream; a nightmare. The terrible dark time was over, and I was overjoyed that I could breathe, overjoyed that I had a second chance; overjoyed that I KNEW God loved me and had healed me. I had never felt such love and forgiveness. I had experienced the hand of God. He gave me the miracle of beginning my life again, new and fresh.

Chapter Fifteen: Looking back and growing day by day

Looking back on my life since those awful days, I realize that I've grown so much. In fact, each time I've gone through deep trials, I see that God's mighty hand has been on me, protecting me and teaching me.

Will I experience deep sorrows in my life again? Yes. Will I go through heartache again? Yes. Will the Lord forsake me during the tough times? Never.

The truth is, His mercies are new every day. Because of His grace, we live our lives with His Holy Spirit guiding us and loving us through the good times and the bad. Most of all, when our time on this earth is over, our last breath here will be our first breath in Heaven. We will see Him face to face, and we will live our eternal life praising and worshiping Him.

Chapter Sixteen: In closing

We must keep our eyes focused on the Lord, and confess our sins daily. We must stay in the Word, and try to live our lives pleasing Him.

His Word gives us instructions for every life problem we'll face, and shares with us how others in Biblical days struggled just as we do.

Throughout the Book of Psalms, we read how many times David cried out to the Lord. His life story is a true example of how we should cry out to the Lord. God heard his cries then, just as He hears our cries today.

Take for example, in Psalm 28:2, David prayed when he was surrounded by trouble and wickedness: "Hear my cry for mercy as I call to you for help, as I lift up my hands toward your Most Holy Place", and Psalm 28:6-7 says: "Praise be to the Lord, for he has heard my cry for mercy. The Lord is my strength and shield; my heart trusts in him, and I am helped. My heart leaps for joy and I will give thanks to him in song."

In Psalm 61:1-5, we find: "Hear my cry, O God; listen to my prayer. From the ends of the earth I call to you, I call as my heart grows faint; lead me to the rock that is higher than I. For you have been my refuge, a strong tower against the foe. I long to dwell in your tent forever and take refuge in the shelter of your wings."

Psalm 62:5-8 says: "Find rest, O my soul, in God alone: my hope comes from him. He alone is my rock and my salvation; he is my fortress, I will not be shaken. My salvation and my honor depend on God; he is my mighty rock, my refuge. Trust in him at all times, O people; pour out your hearts to him, for God is our refuge."

When times come in our lives, and we have a desire for God's presence, provision, and protection as David did when he wrote in Psalm 63:7-8: "Because you are my help, I sing in the shadow of your wings. My soul clings to you; your right hand upholds me."

Lastly, we connect once again with the words of the Bible in Psalm:121: "I lift up my eyes to the hills- where does my help come from? My help comes from the Lord, the Maker of heaven and earth. He will not let your foot slip- he who watches over you will not slumber; Indeed, he who watches over Israel will neither slumber nor sleep. The Lord watches over you- the Lord is your shade at your right hand; the sun will not harm you by day, nor the moon by night. The Lord will keep you from all harm- he will watch over your life; the Lord will watch over your coming and going both now and forevermore."

(*From the New International Version Life Application Bible)

THE MOUNTAIN
BY LORI B. MOORE

There was a land, a very special land,
where all you could see was beauty,
fashioned from God's hand.

Far out on the horizon, God took extra time to create one special mountain;
it was the tall one; the one everyone could see from a distance-
the one everyone admired.

God gave the majestic mountain beautiful tall trees, waterfalls,
and all types of flowers and creatures made it their home.

So it was, year after year, millennia after millennia,
the mountain, so proud and strong, would watch the seasons
come and go, and come and go...

Summer would find new growth on the trees, warm sunshine would bathe the
mountain, and birds would sing in the tree branches that swayed in the
summer breeze.

In autumn, the mountain was especially proud and happy, when all the
colorful leaves on the trees would cover the slopes like a beautiful quilt.

Winter was quiet, and peaceful...the great mountain covered in a blanket of
white softness and he was so content.

Then spring would bring renewal, seeds would sprout, and once again new growth appeared-leaves-tulips-beautiful beyond compare.

The mountain thought, "I am so blessed. Thank You, God, for the gift of strength and endurance. Nothing, not fire nor earthquake, could ever affect me. You've set me apart-I'm Your highest and mightiest mountain.

But...,one day, when the winter snows had melted, and the tulips were once again beginning to sprout from the fertile ground, the mighty mountain heard strange noises, loud engines, saws, and voices.

Much to his dismay, loud thunderous blasts began, and he watched, and felt pain, as chunk, after rock, after slope began to crumble from his beautiful sides.

Until, one day, the mountain was stripped bare-cold-silent-broken-and sad. He had watched the destruction unfold, and mighty as he was, he was powerless-unable to speak-unable to stop it.

"Oh, how could this be?" the mountain cried. "I was tall and strong, You fashioned me that way, Lord. How could You stand by and allow this to happen-to me-if You loved me?"

When the mountain could cry no more, God spoke, "My beautiful, special one. you can restore your beauty and dignity. The inside of you is still mighty and strong. You're broken, yes, but if you choose, you can rebuild, and I'll help you-step by step."

The mountain realized how very much he needed God, and most of all, that God still loved him-broken and all.

Then the mountain watched as God unfolded His mighty arms, spoke the words, and the miracle began to unfold.

God sent the wind that sprinkled the parched and empty mountain sides with seeds of hope. He sent rain to nourish and revive the soil, and rays of golden sunlight to heal his wounds.

Birds, squirrels, foxes, and furry rabbits began to scurry through his grassy slopes once again, and...

Little by little-day by day-God held him and molded him until he was a stronger and more beautiful mountain than ever before.

This time, the mighty mountain sighed, and deeply humbled, said, "God, from now on, each flower that blooms, I'll cherish; each season I'll welcome with awe and amazement, and always in doing so, I'll remember that You never told me I would not be hit by storms, or have trees toppled by adversity.

"Most of all, Lord, I thank You that You never left me; that You rebuilt me and made me whole and stronger than ever before..."

Once again, the mountain stood tall, great and beautiful beyond compare. Great-yet humble; mighty-but profoundly grateful, and he gave thanks to the Lord, for he knew in his heart that God loved him enough to grow him.

The mountain, and all its creatures, the trees in all their beauty, felt honored that God had chosen them to show the other hills of the land-that no matter what storms they face...

God always promises the warm rays of a golden sun that will rise for them each morning with a new and magnificent beginning.

MY TESTIMONY:
BY STEPHANIE W.

I was raised in the church from day one. Even as a small child I sang in the children's choir. I went to Sunday School, to church, and as a teenager I was involved with the youth group.

This continued as an adult, and every time the doors were open I was there. I sang in adult choir, served on church committees, and volunteered many years to serve as choir director. I served on the church board and took every Bible study that was offered at my church. I was sponsored and did a weekend spiritual retreat.

However, even with all I did at church, I had a big empty hole in the center of me that I could never fill.

I had felt this from the time I can remember. For my kindergarten and first grade years my family lived in Nashville. I loved where we lived and enjoyed school. I had friends to play with on my street. We played outside and at each other's homes.

The summer between my first and second grades, we moved to the country in rural Williamson County, but I still went to the city schools in Franklin. Franklin was a very "uppity" hard town to move to, or at least at that time it was to me.

I was an outsider, an outcast, a "foreigner", and it was painful. I simply felt like I didn't fit anywhere.

I was a loner. It was safer that way because then no one could find fault in what I said, what I wore, or what I did if I just stayed quiet.

I was miserable going to school in Franklin, but I didn't feel like I had any options. It was just the way it was. I kept my thoughts a secret from my family; about how awful it was.

We lived on a dead-end street, and there were no other girls on my street. When we first moved there, besides my brother and me, there was a teenage boy who lived across the street.

Playing football in his front yard one day, turned into being sexually abused five times, however, I didn't understand that it was abuse at the time.

I didn't understand that it was abuse, and I still have a hard time understanding. I was an eight-year-old little girl, and wasn't old enough to make adult decisions. For years I blamed myself for not saying "no". I kept this secret inside until I was forty-four years old. I never told my parents; I never told anyone.

So it was, at eight years old I started living in fear. I felt dirty, and he told me I would get in trouble if I told. He told me that he loved me. I lived with the fear that if my parents found out, I would be rejected. I had it in my head that they wouldn't love me anymore and that it was all my fault.

At age eight, I began to hide from God because I felt dirty and bad.

I also started eating, and couldn't seem to get enough candy, cake, or cookies. If there were leftovers, I ate them. I hid when I ate so no one would say, "You don't need that".

I remember going to my grandmother's house as a little girl, and raiding her cabinets and her refrigerator. When she knew we were coming she would buy more food or make food that I didn't get at home. One time, she made a jam cake, and I ate so much of it that night that I awoke in the middle of the night throwing up. My body couldn't handle it.

I would try to quietly take the plates out of the cabinet, and the knives and forks out of the drawer so no one would know I was in the kitchen. I started gaining weight between eight and nine years old, but I was so active the exercise kept me from being obese.

I never ever felt full. As I grew up, I continued to exercise enough not to have an obesity problem, however that ended when I went to college. As the exercise decreased, the weight increased.

I would diet, lose weight, then gain it back again. It was a never ending yo-yo cycle.

When I graduated from college, I weighed 210 lbs. At 5'8" I carried it well. A few semesters before graduation, a person very close to me tried to commit suicide.

This became another secret I was not to tell. I had to lie or keep silent about things I didn't understand and I needed help. So my next thing to do was to add alcohol. When I drank I could diet, but I would be able to drink more.

Another vice I used was sex. I found what I thought to be love in sex. I just wanted someone to care about me, make me feel safe, and make me feel loved.

During college I had an affair. I know now I just wanted the attention. After college, I began dating a man sixteen years older than me. He was not married, and we dated for eight years- eight years too long. I felt safe in that relationship.

He told me he would not put up with the drinking, so I quit. I was able to have a drink here or there, without a problem. The problem was, the eating took off again and I gained 120 lbs. during that time. I felt miserable. I wanted him to love me, marry me, and make my life perfect.

I was looking for God, in a man. After this relationship ended, I dated a few others, continued to gain weight, and finally decided that dating just wasn't worth it. I had found my love in food.

I would eat from the time I woke up and all day long. I never quit eating. I would hide food in my desk, and hide wrappers under papers in the trash so that others wouldn't see what I had eaten. I would go to the vending machine and purchase several items at a time, and stick them in my pocket so no one would see. If I were going out to dinner, I would eat before I went, eat at the restaurant, and eat again when I got back home. I would do this just to get enough.

All this was happening while I was "busy" at church. I thought that God had just made me fat, and I was content being that way.

When I volunteered as choir director, I stood in front of the whole church pretending to "get it". I smiled, led the music, and put on the face of someone who thought she knew all there was about God and the Bible. I was so empty, but could not understand what the big black hole was in the center of me.

About three years ago, my pastor gave the invitation to those that might be interested in talking about their walk with Christ, if we wanted to do so, we could give him a call. I made that decision, and cancelled the meeting several times, until I finally hurt enough to follow through. I didn't know at the time that God was literally "shoving" me into a better relationship with Him.

After I finally met with my pastor, he was open and honest enough to ask me if I realized that my eating was an addiction, just like alcohol and drugs. I told him, "Yes, but I give up. I've tried everything and I honestly do not care anymore. I'm tired of caring."

Over the next few weeks, the hole in my heart grew bigger, and I started hurting all over and was so sad. He suggested that I attend a twelve-step meeting that focused on eating disorders.

I went to the meeting and realized I wasn't alone anymore. I found out that I wasn't the only person on this earth who couldn't stop eating.

The first step is "I'm powerless over food- and my life is unmanageable". I knew from the beginning I was powerless, yes, but unmanageable? No. Here I was, an independent, hard-working woman with a great job. I knew what everyone else should be doing in their lives. If they would just do what I thought they should do, we would all be happy! I thought I had everything managed!

The second step is "Came to believe in a power greater than ourselves that could restore us to sanity". I had no problem believing in a "power greater than myself", but I wasn't insane.

I had prayed so many times that God would fix my weight. If I could just be the right weight, then my whole life would be perfect. I wanted God to somehow unzip the fat from my body. I didn't want to do the footwork and put the food down. Why couldn't I just eat what I wanted and still be the perfect size?

The third step is "Turned our will and lives over to the care of God as we understood Him". God was too busy for me, and so far I wasn't quite sure where He was. He had bigger things to take care of and I should be able to take care of my issues.

In the literature of my twelve-step program, it talks about those of us who've had a spiritual relationship with God sometimes having a harder time turning to Him. Once I really started looking into my life, I found out just how unmanageable it really was.

I treated people with disrespect and was angry often lashing out at others. I knew more than everyone else. The biggest release was to actually tell someone for the first time, "I don't know". Those words had never come out of my mouth.

I didn't want others to think I was stupid, and not knowing meant to me that I was. I looked at all the things I had resented in my life- my fears, the harm I had done to others, and my sex life. I discovered that I had put on this mask of being tough and in control, when in reality I was scared to death!

The thought of other people discovering that I wasn't in control would boil up inside me, and I needed something to squelch that; food took care of that for me. It would numb things to the point where I didn't feel anything.

I also found out that when you put the food down, there was nothing to mask the emptiness and the hole inside me just pulled me in. I found myself at the bottom in a very deep depression. What I had been doing, mixing myself up in everyone else's business, gave me the ability to not focus on how I felt. In actuality, I felt that I didn't belong. I didn't fit in my family, I didn't fit in at work, I didn't fit in at church- I didn't fit in anywhere, I didn't belong.

Not being drunk on sugar and food made all those feelings stronger. I thought I was the ugliest, most horrible person, and if I didn't fool everyone and they found out what was on the inside of me, then I really would be alone. Yet, I used this as an excuse that men couldn't see through the outside to the inside, and that's why I couldn't find a husband.

The suicidal thoughts really took over. I just didn't want to exist anymore. I didn't want to hurt, and I was hurting so bad. I remember laying on the floor in my hall one night, crying, and writing in my journal, "God, where are you? What have I done so bad to make me hurt this much? Please God, just make this end".

That was the night I made the decision to end it. My plan was to pull my car in the garage the next night and leave it running so I could just go to sleep and not wake up.

I needed answers about heaven, so before I went home the next night, I met with my pastor and started asking questions. The questions I was asking gave him clues that I was in deep trouble. He took my keys and called my parents to come and get me. That night, I opened up to them and told them my secrets. I was hurting so bad that if they rejected me, it couldn't hurt anymore than I already did. Well, they didn't reject me. They had no idea what had happened to me, but they loved me anyway, and then they sought help for me.

My doctor started trying different medication to help rid me of the depression, and I began therapy to deal with the childhood issues. It was important that I no longer use my experiences as a crutch, but instead to get to the point where I could accept what had happened and possibly use my experiences to help others.

Four months later, I was still having trouble hitting rock bottom and I was ready to kill myself again. It was then that my therapist checked me into the hospital. They took me off all medication, and realized that I am one of many people with a chemical imbalance. Once the right medication got into my system, then miracles began to happen.

During all this time, I had had so many feelings and emotions about God. At times I hated Him. I didn't feel that He loved me at all. I thought that I was such a bad person that He had finally had enough of me.

I wondered if I had been the woman at the well with Jesus, would He have simply walked away. I screamed at God so many times during this period, and one night I remember screaming "God, if You are there, just come sit in this chair across from me so we can talk". That did not happen.

Another time I wrote in my journal about my dog I had at that time. She has since died, and that was so sad. She was a sweet dog that I had adopted. She, too, had been abused and was scared of people, yet she wanted to be loved so badly. In my journal notes, I wrote about how much she wanted to be loved, but was too scared to let anyone touch her. She wanted so much to play, but she would suddenly become shy because she was afraid. If she had only known how much I loved her anyway and that I would always be there for her. I would protect her and provide for her.

My mentor asked me when I read her the notes I had written in my journal, "Can you let God love you like you love Jodie?" That was the turning point for finding a God of my understanding.

During the last few years since becoming involved in the twelve-step program, God has placed people in my life who love me when at times I've been unable to love myself. These people are honest, and they hold me accountable. God put these special people in my life to help guide me to a more healthy life spiritually, physically, and mentally. He has relieved me of 120 lbs. I no longer live on the phone interfering in other people's lives. I now have people around me whom I trust not to reject me.

Oh, I still have many fears, but I also have ways to cope with these so that I don't include using food, alcohol, or sex in order to cope. Yes,

I still have a long way to go, but I now go to church to worship, and not to be seen. I'm not so busy at church trying to fill the hole and to try to work my way into heaven.

I'm learning that I'm not stupid, and that I don't have to know everything. I'm learning how to be a servant and be of service to others; not to be so wrapped up in myself. I know that the world doesn't revolve around me.

I still have my ups and downs, but I'm also learning to take each day just as it is. I'm learning to say, "I'm sorry" when I mess up instead of trying to prove that the other person was more wrong than me. I'm learning that I can't be other people's God and that I don't want to be.

Each day is a learning experience. I was angry at first when I realized I had an abnormal relationship with food. However, God used this to keep me alive all these years. He knew when the time was right to give me the gift of the twelve-step program, and He has taught me to be grateful to be a food addict and a compulsive overeater.

The one thing I'm most grateful for are the people I have met and the friends I have made in the program. The relationships I have made with these people are the most honest I've ever had in my life. I realize that if I had not had my addiction to food, I might have never met these wonderful people.

Now I know in my heart that I belong; I finally fit in. Most of the time I know God loves me and I'm learning to love myself. Knowing this allows me to love others in a healthy way.

MY TESTIMONY
BY GABY OVERALL

I was born in Atlanta, and at the age of three I moved to Memphis where I lived my whole life until 2007, when my family moved to Nashville.

My grandmother, aunt, and great-grandmother on my mom's side lived there, and I would come and visit whenever possible.

My father's side of the family lived in Atlanta, where I would visit as well.

When I was nine years old, my dad died while he was at work. I was in the third grade, and it was very, very tough on me. I was the kind of person who would stuff my feelings, and I did so for many years.

My brother, who is four years younger than me, took the news very hard as well.

A few years after dad's death, when I was twelve years old, I came to Nashville to visit my grandmother. I had always gone to church with my aunt, and one night after a church function she led me to the Lord.

I remember this so clearly, and the fact that I grew up going to church every week. I didn't know anything different. I lived a Christian life very well for a few years, until I hit the eighth grade, when something inside me changed.

I started making some bad choices, which led me down the wrong path in many ways. I started hanging out with the wrong kind of people and became a follower instead of a leader. Satan knew my weaknesses and I fell into the temptations he threw at me, which he then used against me.

When I went to high school it all went downhill. My mom took us to church every week, but I pretended for a long time and made excuses for some of the things I was doing. I told myself it was okay if I did these things because it wasn't as bad as it seemed to do so. In reality none of it was right!

As the years progressed I got more and more away from what I knew was right, and before long it became the norm for me.

After high school I worked at a restaurant and got into an even worse crowd. I started making worse decisions and was by now far removed from my church. I still went to church, even though I really wasn't there.

I ended up getting pregnant at age nineteen and had my son at age twenty. That experience changed my life a lot.

I started going back to church more and quit the job at the restaurant. I got away from the bad crowd, but I still didn't change everything.

It wasn't until I got married and we found a great church that I rededicated my life to the Lord, and it was then that my husband got saved. We praise God that we found that church!

We had the most amazing pastor and found so many great Christian friends. I took many classes trying to better myself as a mom and a wife. It wasn't until all this happened that I realized all the years I'd made bad choices, I had done so because I was searching in the wrong place for what I needed.

You see, after my dad died I didn't have a "father" figure in my life. I was searching and longing for the kind of fatherly love that only the Savior Jesus Christ could give. I finally realized all the wrong I had done all those years. If I had just sought the Lord instead of looking to other guys in my life, I would have been so much happier and most likely would not have made some of the bad choices I had made.

I have no regrets in my life now, because I believe the day I got pregnant with my son Corey was the day God saved my life from going in a direction I did not want it to go.

I thank Him all the time for that fact.

Some people may say it was a consequence or regret, but I look at it as the best thing that ever happened to me.

I have asked for forgiveness for all the bad decisions I made in my life, and am so thankful for His forgiveness. One of my favorite quotes is from a lady that mentored me for many years learning about God and His forgiveness. She always said, "It is all under the blood of Christ!"

I am here to tell you today that whatever it is that you have done or will do in the future, "It is all under the blood!" We must never live a life full of regrets.

1 John, 1:9 says, "He is faithful and just to forgive us our sins and cleanse us from all unrighteousness."

You see, the only way to get real fulfillment and passion is in our personal relationship with Jesus. He designed us with a need for Him. If we don't let Him fulfill that need, we start looking for someone or something else to fill it.

The more you know Him, spend time with Him, and allow His love to fill you, the more you will find meaning for your life. If you run from Him you will never have that empty place in your heart filled the right way; you will instead feel forever empty.

Everything in life comes down to one thing- Jesus! If your relationship with Him is first, then the rest will fall into place.

MY TESTIMONY:
BY ANDREA HUDDLESTON

My childhood was one of insecurity and constant change. I never knew what the next twenty-four hours would be like. Would I be alive, would I be sleeping in my own bed, or even at my own house?

I learned early on how to grow up fast and to protect myself. When I was ten years old, I was coming home from school to an empty house.

I would do my homework and get ready for my parents and brother to come home. I ironed my dad's uniform for the next day, made dinner, and cleaned the house.

When my dad got home from work, he expected the house to be quiet, and he would lay on the sofa and watch TV.

On some days he would drink, and if that was the case, the evening would not be good. My mom would come home and fighting would begin. Sometimes he would leave and return once we were in bed, and then it would start all over again.

He would get my mom out of bed, and there would be fighting and crying. I would not be able to go back to sleep. You see, nothing was safe at that point.

Dad slept with a gun, and I was always afraid he would kill us in our sleep, so if I didn't sleep he wouldn't get me without me at least knowing first.

As I got older and started driving, I would stay busy.

I wanted to be loved and I wanted someone to protect me. I found that answer with boyfriends. The problem was I was willing to give everything and they were only wanting a girlfriend.

The first serious relationship lasted a year and a half. He was my first guy, with whom I was sexually active. I knew we would get married, but he went off to college and broke up with me, leaving me left behind to deal with the loss.

I spent the night with a friend and took a bottle of aspirin, then woke up her mom and told her what I had done. I realized I didn't want to die.

My parents said, "How could you do this to us? We have loved you and given you everything. We are never going to talk about this again." You see, that is how it was in my family. It was way too messy to deal with the ugliness.

In my next relationship, we dated about a year. I had a promise ring, but of course, he decided he didn't want me anymore. It was tough, but somehow the Lord brought me through with His help.

There was only one other relationship, but I realized I didn't want to be with him the rest of my life.

Then I was hit with the guilt of not following God's plan. The shame you feel is horrible.

When I met my husband and we both realized we were going to be married someday, I felt I had to talk with him about every relationship I'd had. He had a past also. We both had to forgive , and with lots of counseling we have had a blessed marriage.

What you don't realize is, as life goes on, these former lovers can come back into your life at work, church, or other places. You have to live the rest of your life seeing them and wondering what he thinks, what does his wife think, and what do his children know?

God has a plan for us, and we have to live His plan so the heartache we are left with is not in our lives anymore.

I am a blessed woman with a husband who loves me, and I have four wonderful children. I have tried to raise my children with as much of God's Word and guidance He can give.

KADEN'S STORY
BY TERRI HAGOOD

My heart has always been for children. I remember the times that I had my own babies, and I had this spot in my heart to have a little one around again.

I learned of a ministry at our church about women who were in prison who had given birth without any family or support to care for their children while incarcerated. As a result, state foster care was their only choice until released from prison. That is, until Jonah's Journey came into play.

Jonah's Journey enables women to meet host families that are willing to foster these children, allowing the mothers to continue bonding with their children. The mothers are also mentored and ministered to by these families in hopes that they will make the changes needed in their life and reunite with their children upon release from prison.

So, I began to pray and seek the Lord in my response to the call I was feeling in my heart. I went to my husband and he began to pray, as did my teenage son and daughter.

As my family was in prayer for this ministry, I happened to walk by a table at Long Hollow Baptist Church that featured information on the ministry, Jonah's Journey. I realized that I had to stop and sign up for possible child placement.

After we were approved by the church to receive a child, I received a call that there was a six-month old child they wanted us to take.

Wow, I prayed even harder, and my husband and I felt we should in fact do this. We set up a meeting with the mother and left knowing it was what God wanted us to do.

Two weeks after we brought this child into our home, we were all in love with him. He brought so much joy to us. I had confirmation that this was how I was to serve God at this time in my life.

Going in, we thought it was temporary for a six-month period, after which I was prepared to have the baby returned to his mother upon her anticipated parole. After her hearing, we discovered that she would have to serve the remainder of her sentence and could not receive parole. Bottom line, that would mean we would have the child for the remainder of her full sentence, and it would be another full year. What we anticipated being six months actually became one and a half years on that day.

I have to admit that after leaving the hearing I broke down and cried. I felt like I loved this child, but how could I keep feeling as if I was a babysitter?

Could I realistically do this for another year? As I shed my tears, many thoughts went through my mind. I was encouraged by my friend who had been walking with me through this journey. She reminded me of the verses God gave me early on for this child, 1 Peter 3:8-17, and peace flooded my soul. I was to love this child while I had him, to care for him, and to pray continuously over his life.

The next year we visited the mother in prison with her child almost weekly, and encouraged her. We began to see her heart change. She accepted the Lord's forgiveness and started to grow herself. She made great strides to better herself by getting her GED and took many classes to improve her situation. Many calls, visits, and letters were exchanged, since everyone desired and felt encouraged that she wanted to improve her life.

As the days approached for her release, we began to make plans for her new life. We were all excited and looked forward to her having both hope and a future (Jer. 29:11).

Then release day for her came. Wow, how a year and a half had flown since we first received him. As we waited for her to come out, we were excited and nervous all at the same time. We took her shopping and out to eat while loving on her child. We had found her a place to live, a job, and had agreed to pay for her to continue her education. I have to admit that I was very nervous about handing this child over whom we had cared for most of his life up to this point. My husband and I continued to trust God for his life that lied ahead.

After only five days from her release date from prison, she came to us and asked us if we would adopt him. Yippie, wow! We were not expecting that at all. What a range of emotions I had over a period of days. This child would be with us forever, and we are so blessed to have him in our life.

Months later the adoption was final, and it was as if he was always to be here; God had found his family. All this began because I wanted to serve God!

What is he calling you to do? Whatever it is, do it without hesitation and with expectation. His ways are not our ways, and if you pray that His will be done, and you are obedient, He will take care of the details. All you have to do is seek Him and you will find Him. God is good all the time!

SO PROUD
BY TERRI HAGOOD

I received a phone call early one morning from my daughter, who was in her first year of college. She was upset about some news she had learned about a friend. This friend was pregnant, scared, and afraid to tell her family of this unexpected news. The boyfriend insisted she have an abortion.

My daughter reached out in many ways to her; many people were praying against this.

The story has many more details, but the most important is that the young lady showed up in the abortion clinic, but when her name was called she ran out in tears. God came through!

This young lady and her family are so in love with this healthy little precious baby girl. My daughter's strength and boldness throughout this time was amazing and I was so proud of her. She knew God had her at this college for a specific reason, and this was obvious to her. There is always a better way to resolve unexpected news. First trust Jesus, and then seek prayer from others. God will give you joy!

STEPHANIE'S STORY
BY ALLYSON HAGOOD

Going into my freshman year of college was very scary for me. I had grown up in the same town all my life and gone through school with the majority of the same students from kindergarten to senior year. So moving three and a half hours away and going to college where I didn't know one person terrified me. I also was on scholarship to play soccer, so that also made me very nervous.

The morning before I left for college a friend stopped by my house to pray with me. After she prayed for me and my freshman year of college, she gave me a card that had the verse Joshua 1:9. The verse states, "Have I not commanded you? Be strong and courageous. Do not be afraid; do not be discouraged, for the Lord your God will be with you wherever you go." I have always known that verse, but I have never clung to it like I did at that point of my life. I used it constantly to remind me that I was not alone and that the Lord is always with me no matter what.

After I got all my things moved in, I immediately began two a day practices for soccer. I was with my teammates from the moment I woke up until I went to sleep at night. I became very close with three of my teammates, and we began to do everything together. All four of us were freshman, so we were all trying to figure out how to juggle our school-work and our busy soccer schedule at the same time.

Midway through the semester we were beginning to get the hang of everything our schoolwork and soccer schedule demanded from us. We all continued to become closer friends day by day. Even though I was getting the hang of college, I still missed home and was still not sure why God had placed me at this specific college. Even though I was having fun,

I still felt as if I did not know what God's purpose was for putting me at this school.

Each day I would doubt God a little more and ask myself, "What am I doing? All my friends are at the same school together, my family is three and a half hours away, and to make thing worse, I had just found out I had to have knee surgery in the middle of our soccer season!"

I was becoming very discouraged. Some days I would even catch myself thinking I was stupid for thinking God wanted me here and that I should have gone to school where all my friends went.

I called home almost every day crying to my mom, telling her how much I hated school and just wanted to come home. Her response every time was, "I will pray God shows you why you are there. He has a purpose for you and we are wrong to ever doubt Him." I would always respond telling her I knew that is true, but in the back of my head I would still doubt God.

A few days after my mom had told me that, I was sitting in class waiting for it to start. One of the girls I had become very close to was in that same class with me, and lately I had been noticing some things about her that just didn't seem right. She had been sick a lot and wasn't herself. It was beginning to bother me a little bit. She came running in to class to get there on time.

When she sat down beside me, she looked like she had been crying and was scared to death. I knew I had to ask her what was going on because that just wasn't like her. When I asked her if everything was okay, her response shocked me. She began to cry again, and after a few minutes of crying she told me she was pregnant. When she said that, my body completely froze and my heart felt like it had stopped. I did not know what to say or how to respond to what she had told me. Class started, so we could not talk about it.

My mind began racing, and I had all these different thoughts going through my head. I started praying that God would put someone in her life to help her and to comfort her during this time because I knew she was scared and worried. I prayed for her family and for the health of this unborn child. I think I was almost as scared as she was.

After class was over, my friend and I began walking back to our dorm. She started telling me how her parents did not know and she was scared to tell them. The only ones who knew were me, another one of our friends on our team, and her boyfriend. She did not know what to do, and she was so confused. She was on a soccer scholarship, and she was never one to get in trouble or cause problems while growing up. She was afraid of what others thought and most importantly what her parents thought. I told her I would pray for her and that God would give her peace about this whole situation.

When I got back to my room, I called my mom in tears explaining to her what had happened and telling her to immediately start praying for her and this whole situation. Before we hung up the phone, my mom told me that this could possibly be the reason God placed me at this school. I wanted to believe her, but I knew I was not capable of handling a situation like this. I was not mature enough to be the one to help my friend in the ways she needed it.

Later that night, I was cleaning my room and found the card my friend had given me before I left for school. I reread the verse, and immediately my heart stopped. My mom was right. This could be why God placed me at this school. I began to pray for wisdom, boldness, and courage to help my friend during this time in her life.

Throughout the next few weeks, I read that verse every day to myself. I even wrote it on a piece of paper and gave it to my friend. She hung it in her room as well. My friend was still struggling with what to do about this baby and was still scared. She had not told her parents yet and was getting pressure from some people to not keep the baby.

I prayed nonstop for her, and so did my mom and several other people in my hometown who knew about her situation. She was struggling, and it was affecting everything she did. Finally after hiding the news of her pregnancy, her parents found out about it and it was a relief to get the worry off her shoulders. She still was upset and embarrassed and struggling on what to do with this baby, but knowing that her parents knew and were not angry with her made her feel better.

After months of prayer from so many people, she walked in my room and told me with the biggest, sweetest smile that she was going to keep this baby no matter what. From that moment on, I knew God had placed me at that school and on that soccer team for one reason and one reason only, and that was to walk with her through that long journey. I began to cry with happiness and called my mom in tears to tell her the good news. For the first time ever, I felt like I had witnessed the power of prayer before my own eyes. It was the most amazing feeling ever. The Lord was with me wherever I went, and I will never doubt Him and His plans ever again.

In May 2010, a precious baby girl was born! She was very healthy and such a blessing to everyone. My friend is so thankful for the decision she made and says she doesn't know what she would do without her baby girl. That baby is a blessing from the Lord! Every time I see pictures or visit her and my friend, tears fill my eyes with happiness. I immediately pray to God, thanking Him for being faithful and for never leaving me.

I am so proud of my precious friend for being bold and for trusting God. Even though she was scared of the unknown, the Lord was with her every step of the way. It made my heart smile when I went to visit her at her house right before the baby was born. The verse I had written down and stuck on her mirror at school is now hanging on her mirror at her house. I am so thankful for everyone who prayed for me to be strong and bold and prayed for my friend as well. Without our awesome God and the power of prayer, I do not know where I would be today or where my precious best friend would be either

THE MASTER'S PLAN
A POEM THAT TELLS OF THE PAIN
OF ABORTION AND THE
FORGIVENESS OF GOD)
BY LORI MOORE

If I could turn back, start my life over again;
Blink, and make the pain go away;
Go back to my youth, this Lord I have prayed.

Yet I am held captive, a prisoner, still,
Of a terrible choice I made at sixteen;
Not to abstain.

Had I chosen differently,
Rejoicing I'd be;
Instead of the worry and fear brought by sin.

But, I chose wrong, and my fear came true.
My life changed forever...a life full of tears.
Shame's brought much heartache here;
To myself, my family, and all I hold dear.

The lofty religious spoke gossiping words
In haughty hushed whispers;
As if they thought I didn't hear their words;
Or read their faces, or saw their stares.

You knew the pain I felt, but I'd no one to listen;
No one whom I could share.
You delighted in judging, I was guilty, this was true,
But as fate may have happened, it could have been you.

So lost and alone, I needed a friend to love and assure me;
Help me know I'd get through- the pregnancy-,
And tell me I'd be okay, but not one encouraging word did you say.

I remember that day when crying I said, "Lord, hear me.
Now, which road do I take?
Which life choice should I make?"

Either one's filled with such pain.
Will adoption for my baby be?
To another home?
To another family?

Or shall I choose abortion now and hope I'd easily forget?
Impossible! That memory would be-
That I inside once carried you...my child.

From that day on, innocence was gone;
So quickly lost, never to return.
The scars deep inside my heart
I tried to forget; I tried to erase.

Now as long as my life shall be
I'll cry when I see a loving family.
The wistful thoughts of what could have been.

LORI B. MOORE

A child, my child, you were meant to be.
But your sweet life was cut short...erased...
My secret none would see.

You were never given a chance to laugh and play.
Abortion, I thought you would end my pain.
But still it persists, and even today-
The emptiness...cries...guilt was my gain.

Thinking then I wouldn't be so sad.
But oh, how wrong, how wrong could I be
I'm full of regret, no easy solution did I see.

Now, remembering those days gone by;
At each new sunset, again, I cry;
And my thoughts, away they fly.
Remembering your birthday-because of me,
It would never be.

Yet, on this day I make a choice and choose
Forgiveness for myself.
I will love me as you love me, Lord, and
Gave my life a second chance.

Even though those days have long since passed.
I lay down my sin-
My life at your feet.

Through you, Lord, my life is complete.
I'm healed now, and have a sweet peace,
And freedom from the pain and grief.

I commit the rest of my life to thee.
I realize I have eternal destiny!
Through your grace, your mercy,
And your sweet love;
I'm restored, accepted, redeemed
And amazed.

I'll experience what it will be like to hold you-
On that day in heaven my dream will come true.

I'll see your sweet face, child.
Your life wasn't erased, you lived on in heaven;
And your life, it had meaning.

God took away my shame and guilt
And gave me a promise
Of a new beginning.

Oh, heavenly Father, your love's so amazing.
You are the great potter and we are your children.
and oh, how I realize it now; because you love me
you'll never break that vow.

Lord, nothing will ever tear us apart or take you away.
'Cause the gift you gave me, it came with a price;
Your life given for me, for you love the whole world.
You are our master; your face one day we'll see.

Your hope reigns forever; in us, you have a plan.
Yes, this is true. For one day at our life's end.

No tears will be shed then, you're the light of the world!
So, friend, if you know someone who is hurting,
Remember to gently encourage, draw closer;
Offer a hug, say a prayer, share this gift with another.

Reach out, recite the Master's plan;
Make a difference, envision a little one's hand.
Hear a giggle from a voice not yet heard.
Give a loving embrace;
Help unborn hearts
To keep beating.

MY TESTIMONY
BY RHONDA PONESSA

My parents divorced when I was three years old. My mom remarried when I was six to a wonderful man, Harry Yates. They currently pastor the Nashville Cowboy Church. I was blessed with not one wonderful father, but two.

I grew up in a godly Christian home where I was loved and taught about the Lord. I was saved at a young age, and honestly, I don't remember a time when I didn't know the Lord. I grew up knowing about the Lord and being taught on a daily basis about His love and mercies.

Sometimes when that is the situation, it's difficult to name a specific time and place when you gave your heart to Him. The fact that I didn't have a set salvation date used to bother me because I've heard so many people say, "I remember my big salvation experience."

Many times that caused me to question my own salvation. I didn't have a date, a time, a memorable moment, or this drastic life change like many others did, so I questioned it. God, in all His mercy, showed me several years ago that His promise remains true regardless of my feelings.

We are not to depend on our feelings, but His faithfulness, and that His word is true. Ephesians 2:8 says, "It is by grace you have been saved, not of yourselves, it is the gift of God." I'm so glad that I can rest in that truth.

Mrs. Ruth Graham was a great inspiration to me in that she did not have a date or specific memory of her salvation either, for like me, she was saved at a very young age. It was a slow growing process that changed her life through God. If this is you, I pray that you will also be encouraged by that as I was.

My family has always been involved in music- country music, because my uncle is Johnny Cash. My family and I began a musical evangelistic ministry when I was about nine years old, and we traveled the country by bus. We ministered all over the world, preaching, and singing God's word.

I led an amazing young life and was able to experience so many things that young people my age only dream of. I feel so blessed to have been given those opportunities.

By the time I was thirteen years old, I had been to eight different countries, I had stood on the stage of the Grand Old Opry, and I had recorded several albums. I experienced so much more than most people do in a lifetime.

But, as I grew I knew the Lord had plans for me personally, and at seventeen years of age I got off the road to find my own way and to see the Lord's direction for my life.

I moved in with my aging grandparents, Grandmother and Grandfather Cash at the request of my Uncle Johnny to help care for them. This was a very special time for me.

My parents were still traveling on the road, so being with my grandmother was such a blessing and a comfort to me. My grandmother and I were always close, but these two years together allowed me to make some special memories that helped mold me into the person I am today. God used my grandmother to direct and guide me in so many ways. She taught me to play the piano, which she played beautifully by ear, and to keep me eyes on Jesus even in the difficult times. I still miss her every day, even though it's been almost twenty years since her passing.

Over the years I have used the voice God has given me to glorify Him, singing solos, and singing in a gospel trio Adoration. I also do vocal recording backup work. Along with my singing, I do interior design work as time allows.

I am happily married to a wonderful man who loves me, our family, and loves the Lord. We have a fifteen-year-old daughter who is the joy of our lives. I am truly blessed!

As I reflect back on my life, I can see God's hand guiding me even when I didn't feel it or when I was straying away from Him. He was and is always there, as He will be for anyone who calls on His name.

Deuteronomy 4:29 tells us that when we seek the Lord, we will find Him if you look for Him with all your heart. Hebrews 8:12 says that He will forgive our wickedness and will remember our sins no more. What a feeling that is!

I pray that my testimony will be used for his glory and help someone find the peace and joy that only comes with knowing the Lord Jesus Christ.

CONCLUSION:

Hopefully, your heart has been touched by reading The Power of a Testimony. Perhaps the testimonies in this book have given you God's gift of peace or encouraged you to share your story with others so they may come to know His transforming love.

You have been lifted up in the knowledge that you were not alone in past suffering and you are a new creation in Christ Jesus today.

I had many reasons to comprise this book. One in particular was to show that we no longer have to be oppressed by walls of shame and secrecy. By sharing our testimony and how He saved us we show others how Christ restores and forgives all of those that call on His name.

If we can reach even one person and are able to make a difference in their life by sharing our life stories, then we have made a difference for the Kingdom of God.

All of us are significant to God. Remember when Jesus tells the Parable of the Lost Sheep in Luke 15:3-7, "Suppose one of you has a hundred sheep and loses one of them. Does he not leave the ninety-nine in the open country and go after the lost sheep until he finds it? And when he finds it, he joyfully puts it on his shoulders and goes home. Then he calls his friends and neighbors together and says, 'Rejoice with me; I have found my lost sheep.' I tell you that in the same way there will be more rejoicing in heaven over one sinner who repents than over ninety-nine righteous persons who do not need to repent."

Our Savior is full of compassion, love, mercy, and grace. He has given each of us a plan and a purpose. Ask Christ to reveal to you your purpose and His plan for your life. Trust in Him, step out in obedience to His call, and stand amazed as He equips you for the task.

As I conclude this book, I am filled with a sense of freedom and peace. I never knew that writing my testimony would lead me to have a desire to write a book. I had only decided to write down my experience at seventeen in hopes that I could find peace and hopefully let go of the pain of my teen pregnancy.

Lord, I stand amazed! Looking back on this journey, You had a plan and a purpose in all of the painful times back then to use it for Your glory today.

I know the times in my life when I have made poor choices my thoughts have taken me back to that time long ago when I called out to You and You answered me. I am so grateful that I serve a God of second and third chances!

We continue to pray to You, Lord, to cleanse us from the inside out. May we never forget our salvation experience, and like the Biblical David in Psalm 51:10-12,

"Create in me a pure heart, O God, and renew a steadfast spirit within me. Do not cast me from your presence or take your Holy Spirit from me. Restore to me the joy of your salvation, and grant me a willing spirit, to sustain me."

I join you in praying that we become a society of truth, transparency, forgiveness, and love and may we honor the Lord by serving Him.

Made in United States
Orlando, FL
11 June 2023

34044165R00055